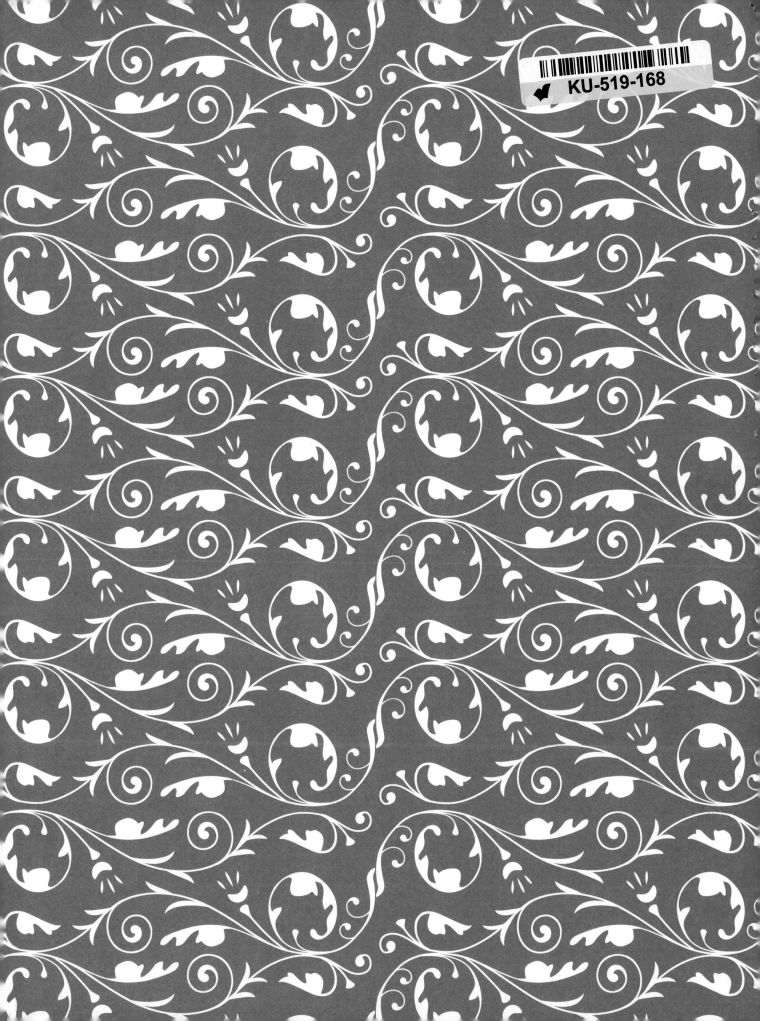

# Christmas Food

# Christmas Food

Love Food ® is an imprint of Parragon Books Ltd

Parragon
Queen Street House
4 Queen Street
Bath BA1 1HE, UK

ISBN: 978-1-4075-3398-8
Printed in China

Designed and produced by the Bridgewater Book Company Ltd

The publisher would like to thank the following for permission to reproduce copyright material:
Lisa Thornberg/iStockphoto: 6; Jurga Rubinovaite/iStockphoto: 7.

Notes for the Reader
This book uses both imperial and metric measurements. Follow the same units of measurement throughout; do not mix imperial and metric. All spoon measurements are level: teaspoons are assumed to be 5 ml and tablespoons are assumed to be 15 ml. Unless otherwise stated, milk is assumed to be full fat, eggs and individual vegetables such as potatoes are medium and pepper is freshly ground black pepper. Recipes using raw or very lightly cooked eggs should be avoided by infants, the elderly, pregnant women, convalescents and anyone suffering from an illness. The times given are an approximate guide only.

# Contents

Introduction: the
*Christmas Feast* 6

Ideas for
*Decorations* 8

Starters, Brunches &
*Lunches* 12

Main Courses &
*Accompaniments* 24

Party Food & *Drinks* 62

Desserts &
*After-dinner Treats* 78

Index 96

# Introduction: the *Christmas Feast*

Christmas is traditionally a time of sharing, a chance to relax in the company of your family and friends and, perhaps, to treat yourself a little as well. Hosting the perfect Christmas meal is a wonderful opportunity to enjoy all of these experiences.

Christmas dinner is, for many people, one of the highlights of the festive season. In today's fast-paced world, the simple act of sitting down to a home-cooked meal with friends and family has become a rare pleasure, but Christmas remains one of the best occasions to do just that. However, cooking a traditional Christmas meal can often seem like an intimidating task, and this book aims to dispel these anxieties by demonstrating how to prepare many classic festive dishes, plus a host of delicious, modern alternatives.

While planning a Christmas meal isn't complicated, the more forethought you give it, the easier it will be. The key is to do as much ahead of time as you can, to let you enjoy the big day. Bear in mind that Christmas cake and pudding can be made months ahead and are all the better for it, so set aside an afternoon for baking and roll up your sleeves.

Draw up your menu some time in advance and try to choose many dishes that are both delicious and straightforward. Choose recipes that can be made ahead of time or that require just a little heating right before the feast to be completed. Another thing to remember when planning your menu is never choose a recipe that you have not tried before. Select reliable favourites, or, if you would like to add a new dish to your traditional menu, practise making it beforehand.

Set the table and get your home ready a day or two before - this leaves time to borrow or buy anything

extra you may need. A buffet service is easier to manage than seating everyone at the same table. Set the table against a wall to use it as the serving area, and divide the food into small portions.

A beautifully set table can make your meal look even more elegant and inviting, and you don't need to spend a lot of money to do it. Tablecloths cover a multitude of sins while adding colour and pattern. Squares of silk can make a dramatic statement when artfully draped over a plain white tablecloth.

Over the following pages, you will find instructions on how to make decorative napkin holders, which add charm and character to your table setting. There are also instructions for making a Christmas wreath, which can be used as a traditional trimming for your front door or even as a table decoration.

On the day of the feast, remember that food takes longer to cook when there are several dishes in the oven at the same time, so it's better to cook some food ahead and keep it warm so all the dishes will be hot. One handy tip is to line roasting trays with foil and discard at the end of cooking to make washing

up easier, and to clear up as you go along to avoid accumulating a mountain of pots and pans.

Preparing the traditional turkey or goose is probably the most complex part of the festive planning. The number of people you can feed with a particular bird will depend on how meaty it is, but as a rule of thumb a small turkey or goose will serve 4 to 7 people, a medium one 8 to 11, a large one 12 to 15, and an extra-large turkey (over 8 kg/17 lb 10 oz) will serve up to 20. For frozen birds, defrost in the fridge, allowing 18 hours per 1 kg/2 lb 4 oz, or in a cool place for 7 hours per 1 kg/2 lb 4 oz.

Cook the turkey up to an hour in advance and keep it warm by wrapping it in a double layer of foil, then cover it with a tea towel while the other dishes are cooking to avoid last-minute panic. Let the meat rest for at least 30 minutes before carving – this lets the juices settle back into the meat, making it more succulent and easier to carve.

Remember to set aside time for yourself, so that you too can enjoy the fruits of your labour, and have a relaxed and magical Christmas day.

# Festive
# *Napkin Holders*

## MATERIALS

craft wire – thick (2 mm/$\frac{1}{16}$ inch)
    and thin
ready-made solid napkin ring
beige thick cotton fabric
sewing needle and beige strong
    cotton thread
beads of your choice
ribbons to match or coordinate
    with the beads and fabric
white Velcro™
scissors, long-nosed pliers,
    tape measure, tailor's chalk,
    strong double-sided tape,
    extra-strong iron-on hemming
    tape, steam iron

★ Lay the thick craft wire across the width of the napkin ring, then bend it at a right angle around the ring until it is about 3.5 cm/1$\frac{3}{8}$ inches away from the right-angled bend. Bend the wire at a right angle across the ring, then again at a right angle round the other side of the ring in the other direction until you reach the beginning of the wire. Cut the wire, leaving enough surplus to twist the ends together with the pliers. Repeat for the number of napkin holders you require.

★ Measure the width and length of one of the napkin holders and add 1.5 cm/$\frac{5}{8}$ inch to each measurement. Cut two pieces of beige fabric this size for each napkin holder. On one of each pair of fabric pieces, use tailor's chalk to mark the measurements of the napkin holder, centred. Pierce through the fabric at each corner with a needle so that you can see its position on the other side.

★ On the needle-pricked side of the fabric, place double-sided tape along both lengths and widths, flush to the edges. Trim the corners for a neat finish. Align a napkin holder with the pricked holes at one end. Remove the tape backing and fold the fabric edges over the wire to secure. Using the iron-on hemming tape and following the manufacturer's instructions, hem the edges of the second piece of fabric so that it is 5 mm/$\frac{1}{4}$ inch smaller all round than the napkin holder.

★ Thread the beads on to a length of the thin wire, then wrap around the napkin holder. Pierce the ends through the fabric and fold over firmly to ensure that the beads are held securely and the wire doesn't protrude. Wrap the ribbon around, securing it at the back with double-sided tape. Back the napkin holder with the second hemmed piece of fabric, using thin strips of Velcro™ for easy removal.

# Christmas Door
# *Wreath*

## MATERIALS

plain deep-red fabric, red gingham
   and ruby raw-silk fabric, each
   2.5 cm x 1.5 metres/1 inch x
   59 inches
polystyrene wreath 24 cm/
   9½ inches in diameter
red gingham 2.5 cm x 50 cm/
   1 inch x 20 inches
21 holly leaves, 16 about 6 cm/
   2½ inches in length and 5 about
   4 cm/1½ inches in length
floristry wire
2 fir cones on wire about 5 cm/
   2 inches in length
fake berries on flexible stems
tape measure, scissors,
   strong double-sided tape,
   long-nosed pliers

★ Wrap the red fabric strip around the wreath – the point at which you start and finish will become the bottom of the wreath. Use double-sided tape to secure the ends. Do not worry about covering all the polystyrene at this stage.

★ Repeat with the larger length of gingham, starting and ending in the same place and focusing on covering more of the polystyrene. Repeat with the raw silk to cover the remaining polystyrene.

★ Wrap the smaller piece of gingham over where the other strips started and ended as many times as possible, tying the ends in a tight knot. Trim the ends. Use the scissors to trim any stray threads.

★ Thread all the holly leaves with the floristry wire, using the pliers to help direct the wire into the main veins of the holly. The smaller leaves should be together. Use the pliers to pierce all around the polystyrene wreath and insert the large holly leaves into the holes. The smaller leaves should be by the wrapped gingham.

★ Gently push the fir cones under the wrapped gingham with the berries, and finish with the smaller wired holly in between. Push a length of wire into the back of the wreath to make a loop to hang the wreath.

# Starters, Brunches & *Lunches*

# Festive Prawn
## *Cocktail*

**SERVES 8**

125 ml/4 fl oz tomato ketchup
1 tsp chilli sauce
1 tsp Worcestershire sauce
1 kg/2 lb 4 oz cooked tiger prawns
2 ruby grapefruits
lettuce leaves, shredded
2 avocados, peeled, stoned
    and diced

MAYONNAISE
2 large egg yolks
1 tsp English mustard powder
1 tsp salt
300 ml/10 fl oz groundnut oil
1 tsp white wine vinegar
pepper

TO GARNISH
lime slices
fresh dill sprigs

★ First make the mayonnaise. Put the egg yolks in a bowl, add the mustard powder, pepper to taste and salt and beat together well. Pour the oil into a jug and make sure that your bowl is secure on the work surface by sitting it on a damp cloth. Using an electric or hand whisk, begin to whisk the egg yolks, adding just 1 drop of the oil. Make sure that this has been thoroughly absorbed before adding another drop and whisking well.

★ Continue adding the oil 1 drop at a time until the mixture thickens and stiffens - at this point, whisk in the vinegar and then continue to dribble in the remaining oil very slowly in a thin stream, whisking constantly, until you have used up all the oil and you have a thick mayonnaise.

★ Mix the mayonnaise, tomato ketchup, chilli sauce and Worcestershire sauce together in a small bowl. Cover with clingfilm and refrigerate until required.

★ Remove the heads from the prawns and peel off the shells, leaving the tails intact. Slit along the length of the back of each prawn with a sharp knife and remove and discard the dark vein. Cut off a slice from the top and bottom of each grapefruit, then peel off the skin and all the white pith. Cut between the membranes to separate the segments.

★ When ready to serve, make a bed of shredded lettuce in the base of 8 glass dishes. Divide the prawns, grapefruit segments and avocados between them and spoon over the mayonnaise dressing. Serve the cocktails garnished with lime slices and dill sprigs.

# Turkey Club
# *Sandwiches*

**SERVES 6**

**SANDWICHES**
12 pancetta or streaky
    bacon rashers
18 slices white bread
12 slices cooked turkey
    breast meat
3 plum tomatoes, sliced
6 Little Gem lettuce leaves
12 stuffed olives
salt and pepper

**MAYONNAISE**
2 large egg yolks
1 tsp English mustard powder
1 tsp salt
300 ml/10 fl oz groundnut oil
1 tsp white wine vinegar
pepper

★ First make the mayonnaise. Put the egg yolks in a bowl, add the mustard powder, pepper to taste and salt and beat together well. Pour the oil into a jug and make sure that your bowl is secure on the work surface by sitting it on a damp cloth. Using an electric or hand whisk, begin to whisk the egg yolks, adding just 1 drop of the oil. Make sure that this has been thoroughly absorbed before adding another drop and whisking well.

★ Continue adding the oil 1 drop at a time until the mixture thickens and stiffens – at this point, whisk in the vinegar and then continue to dribble in the remaining oil very slowly in a thin stream, whisking constantly, until you have used up all the oil and you have a thick mayonnaise. Cover and refrigerate while you prepare the other sandwich components.

★ Grill or fry the pancetta until crisp, drain on kitchen paper and keep warm. Toast the bread until golden, then cut off the crusts.

★ You will need 3 slices of toast for each sandwich. For each sandwich, spread the first piece of toast with a generous amount of mayonnaise, top with 2 slices of turkey, keeping the edges neat, and then top with a couple of slices of tomato. Season to taste with salt and pepper. Add another slice of toast and top with 2 pancetta rashers and 1 lettuce leaf. Season to taste again with salt and pepper, add a little more mayonnaise, then top with the final piece of toast. Cut the sandwich in half. Push a cocktail stick or a decorative sparkler through a stuffed olive, and then push this through the sandwich to hold it together.

# Smoked Salmon

## *Risotto*

**SERVES 4**

50 g/1¾ oz unsalted butter
1 onion, finely chopped
½ small fennel bulb,
   very finely chopped
500 g/1 lb 2 oz arborio or
   carnaroli rice
300 ml/10 fl oz white wine
   or vermouth
1.2 litres/2 pints hot fish stock
150 g/5½ oz hot smoked
   salmon flakes
150 g/5½ oz smoked
   salmon slices
2 tbsp fresh chervil leaves or
   chopped flat-leaf parsley
salt and pepper

★ Melt half the butter in a large saucepan over a medium heat, add the onion and fennel and cook, stirring frequently, for 5-8 minutes until transparent and soft. Add the rice and stir well to coat the grains in the butter. Cook, stirring, for 3 minutes, then add the wine, stir and leave to simmer until most of the liquid has been absorbed.

★ With the stock simmering in a separate saucepan, add 1 ladleful to the rice and stir well. Cook, stirring constantly, until nearly all the liquid has been absorbed before adding another ladleful of stock. Continue to add the remaining stock in the same way until the rice is cooked al dente and most or all of the stock has been added.

★ Remove from the heat and stir in the two types of salmon and the remaining butter, season to taste with salt and pepper and serve scattered with the chervil or parsley.

**COOK'S NOTE**
★ This risotto can be made with cooked prawns or other seafood - try it with crabmeat and saffron.

# Roast Squash with *Cranberries*

SERVES 4

4 acorn or small butternut squash
100 g/3½ oz basmati rice
50 g/1¾ oz wild rice
25 g/1 oz butter
1 tbsp olive oil, plus extra
    for oiling
1 red onion, thinly sliced
2 garlic cloves, crushed
100 g/3½ oz dried cranberries
50 g/1¾ oz pine kernels, toasted
2 tbsp fresh parsley,
    finely chopped
whole nutmeg, for grating
70 g/2½ oz fresh white or
    wholemeal breadcrumbs
25 g/1 oz Parmesan cheese,
    finely grated
butter, for dotting
salt and pepper

★ If using acorn squash, cut through the centre and trim the stalk and root so that the squash will stand upright securely, then scoop out and discard the seeds. If using butternut squash, cut lengthways in half and scoop out and discard the seeds. Place the prepared squash on an oiled baking sheet.

★ Cook the two types of rice separately according to the packet instructions and drain well.

★ Meanwhile, preheat the oven to 190°C/375°F/Gas Mark 5. Melt the butter with the oil in a frying pan over a medium heat, add the onion and garlic and cook, stirring frequently, for 8 minutes, or until transparent and soft.

★ Tip all the cooked rice and the cooked onion and garlic into a bowl. Add the cranberries, pine kernels and parsley, grate in a little nutmeg and season to taste with salt and pepper. Mix together well.

★ Carefully divide the stuffing mixture between the squash, then top with the breadcrumbs and Parmesan cheese and dot with butter. Bake in the preheated oven for 50 minutes, then serve hot.

**COOK'S NOTE**

★ You can vary the stuffing ingredients and use other nuts such as walnuts or almonds and replace the cranberries with chopped ready-to-eat dried apricots.

# Double Cheese
## *Souffles*

**MAKES 6**

25 g/1 oz butter, plus extra
   for greasing
2 tbsp finely grated Parmesan
   cheese
175 ml/6 fl oz milk
25 g/1 oz self-raising flour
whole nutmeg, for grating
100 g/3½ oz soft goat's cheese
70 g/2½ oz mature Cheddar
   cheese, grated
2 large eggs, separated
salt and pepper

★ Preheat the oven to 200°C/400°F/Gas Mark 6. Put a baking sheet in the oven to warm. Generously grease the inside of 6 small ramekins with butter, add half the Parmesan cheese and shake to coat the butter.

★ Warm the milk in a small saucepan. Melt the remaining butter in a separate saucepan over a medium heat. Add the flour, stir well to combine and cook, stirring, for 2 minutes until smooth. Add a little of the warmed milk and stir until absorbed. Continue to add the milk a little at a time, stirring constantly, until you have a rich, smooth sauce. Season to taste with salt and pepper, and grate in a little nutmeg. Add the cheeses to the sauce and stir until well combined and melted.

★ Remove from the heat and leave the sauce to cool a little, then add the egg yolks and stir to combine. In a separate bowl, whisk the egg whites until stiff. Fold a tablespoonful of the egg whites into the cheese sauce, then gradually fold in the remaining egg whites. Spoon into the prepared ramekins and scatter over the remaining Parmesan cheese.

★ Place the ramekins on the hot baking sheet and bake in the preheated oven for 15 minutes until puffed up and brown. Remove from the oven and serve immediately. The soufflés will collapse quite quickly when taken from the oven, so have your serving plates ready to take them to the table.

**COOK'S NOTE**

★ You can vary the cheeses, but always choose a full-flavoured, hard cheese to complement the goat's cheese.

# Main Courses &

## Accompaniments

# Roast Turkey with
## *Bread Sauce*

**SERVES 8**

1 quantity Chestnut and
    Sausage Stuffing
one 5-kg/11-lb turkey
40 g/1½ oz butter

**BREAD SAUCE**
1 onion, peeled
4 cloves
600 ml/1 pint milk
115 g/4 oz fresh white
    breadcrumbs
55 g/2 oz butter
salt and pepper

★ Preheat the oven to 220°C/425°F/Gas Mark 7. If you are planning on stuffing the turkey, spoon the stuffing into the neck cavity and close the flap of skin with a skewer. If you prefer to cook the stuffing separately, cook according to the recipe's instructions.

★ Place the bird in a large roasting tin and rub it all over with the butter. Roast in the preheated oven for 1 hour, then lower the oven temperature to 180°C/350°F/Gas Mark 4 and roast for a further 2½ hours. You may need to pour off the fat from the roasting tin occasionally.

★ Meanwhile, make the bread sauce. Stud the onion with the cloves, then place in a saucepan with the milk, breadcrumbs and butter. Bring just to boiling point over a low heat, then remove from the heat and leave to stand in a warm place to infuse. Just before serving, remove the onion and cloves and reheat the sauce gently, beating well with a wooden spoon. Season to taste with salt and pepper.

★ Check that the turkey is cooked by inserting a skewer or the point of a sharp knife into the thigh - if the juices run clear, it is ready. Transfer the bird to a carving board, cover loosely with foil and leave to rest.

★ Carve the turkey and serve with the warm bread sauce and stuffing.

# Yuletide Goose with
## *Honey & Pears*

SERVES 4–6

one 3.5–4.5-kg/7¾-10-lb
   oven-ready goose
1 tsp salt
4 pears
1 tbsp lemon juice
4 tbsp butter
2 tbsp honey

✱ Preheat the oven to 220°C/425°F/Gas Mark 7. Rinse the goose and pat dry. Use a fork to prick the skin all over, then rub with the salt. Place the bird upside down on a rack in a roasting tin. Roast in the preheated oven for 30 minutes. Drain off the fat. Turn the bird over and roast for 15 minutes. Drain off the fat.

✱ Reduce the heat to 180°C/350°F/Gas Mark 4 and roast for 15 minutes per 450 g/1 lb. Cover with foil 15 minutes before the end of the cooking time. Check that the bird is cooked by inserting a knife between the legs and body. If the juices run clear, it is cooked. Remove from the oven. Transfer the goose to a warmed serving platter, cover loosely with foil and leave to rest.

✱ Peel and halve the pears, then brush with the lemon juice. Melt the butter and honey in a saucepan over a low heat, then add the pears. Cook, stirring, for 5-10 minutes until tender. Remove from the heat, arrange the pears around the goose and pour the sweet juices over the bird, then serve.

**COOK'S NOTE**

✱ 'Christmas is coming and the goose is getting fat' - and they do look like extremely big birds. However, there is proportionately a lot less meat on a goose than on a turkey or chicken because a goose's rib cage is so large.

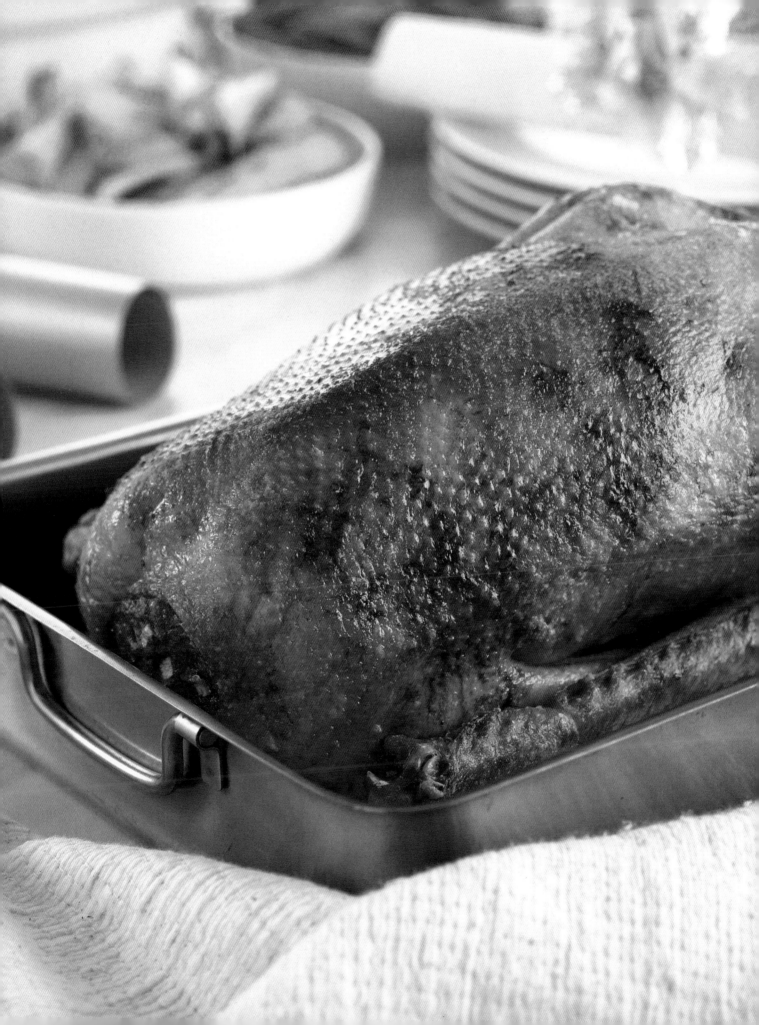

# Roast Pheasant with
## *Wine & Herbs*

SERVES 4

100 g/3½ oz butter,
   slightly softened
1 tbsp chopped fresh thyme
1 tbsp chopped fresh parsley
2 oven-ready young pheasants
4 tbsp vegetable oil
125 ml/4 fl oz red wine
salt and pepper
game chips (see Cook's Note,
   below), to serve

★ Preheat the oven to 190°C/375°F/Gas Mark 5. Put the butter in a small bowl and mix in the chopped herbs. Lift the skins off the pheasants, taking care not to tear them, and push the herb butter under the skins. Season to taste with salt and pepper. Pour the oil into a roasting tin, add the pheasants and roast in the preheated oven for 45 minutes, basting occasionally. Remove from the oven, pour over the wine, then return to the oven and cook for a further 15 minutes, or until cooked through. Check that each bird is cooked by inserting a knife between the legs and body. If the juices run clear, they are cooked.

★ Remove the pheasants from the oven, cover loosely with foil and leave to rest for 15 minutes. Serve on a warmed serving platter surrounded with game chips.

**COOK'S NOTE**

★ To make game chips, peel 650 g/1 lb 7 oz potatoes and cut into wafer-thin slices. Immediately place in a bowl of cold water. Heat sunflower or corn oil in a deep-fryer to 190°C/375°F, or until a cube of day-old bread browns in 30 seconds. Drain the potato slices and pat dry with kitchen paper. Deep-fry, in batches, for 2-3 minutes, stirring to prevent them from sticking, and remove with a slotted spoon. Drain on kitchen paper and keep warm while you cook the remaining slices.

# Duck with Madeira &
## *Blueberry Sauce*

SERVES 4

4 duck breasts (skin left on)
4 garlic cloves, chopped
grated rind and juice of 1 orange
1 tbsp chopped fresh parsley
salt and pepper

MADEIRA AND
BLUEBERRY SAUCE
150 g/5½ oz blueberries
250 ml/9 fl oz Madeira
1 tbsp redcurrant jelly

TO SERVE
new potatoes
selection of green vegetables

★ Use a sharp knife to make several shallow diagonal cuts in each duck breast. Put the duck in a glass bowl with the garlic, orange rind and juice, and the parsley. Season to taste with salt and pepper and stir well. Turn the duck in the mixture until thoroughly coated. Cover the bowl with clingfilm and leave in the refrigerator to marinate for at least 1 hour.

★ Heat a dry, non-stick frying pan over a medium heat. Add the duck breasts and cook for 4 minutes, then turn them over and cook for a further 4 minutes, or according to taste. Remove from the heat, cover the frying pan and leave to stand for 5 minutes.

★ Halfway through the cooking time, put the blueberries, Madeira and redcurrant jelly into a separate saucepan. Bring to the boil. Reduce the heat and simmer for 10 minutes, then remove from the heat.

★ Slice the duck breasts and transfer to warmed serving plates. Serve with the sauce poured over and accompanied by new potatoes and a selection of green vegetables.

**COOK'S NOTE**

★ Duck has a reputation for being a very fatty meat, but modern breeders are producing much leaner birds these days. The meat, therefore, needs careful cooking to prevent it from drying out and losing its texture.

# Chicken
## Roulades

**SERVES 6**

6 skinless, boneless chicken
   breasts, about 175 g/6 oz each
200 g/7 oz fresh chicken mince
1 tbsp olive oil
2 shallots, roughly chopped
1 garlic clove, crushed
150 ml/5 fl oz double cream
3 fresh sage leaves, chopped
1 tbsp chopped fresh parsley
1 tbsp cognac or sherry
1 tbsp vegetable oil
18 pancetta rashers
1 dessertspoon plain flour
200 ml/7 fl oz white wine
200 ml/7 fl oz chicken stock
salt and pepper

**TO SERVE**
Parsnip and Potato Rösti
gravy

✷ Place a chicken breast between 2 pieces of clingfilm and, using a rolling pin, flatten the breast as evenly as possible. Trim off the rough edges to make a neat square. Repeat with the remaining breasts, cover and chill in the refrigerator.

✷ Meanwhile, chop the chicken trimmings and mix with the mince in a bowl. Heat the olive oil in a small frying pan over a medium heat, add the shallots and garlic and cook, stirring frequently, for 5 minutes. Add to the mince with the cream, herbs and cognac and mix together thoroughly. Season to taste with salt and pepper, cover and chill in the refrigerator for 15 minutes.

✷ Bring a large saucepan of water to the boil, then reduce to a simmer. Divide the mince mixture between the breasts, spread to within 1 cm/½ inch of the edge, and then roll each breast up to form a sausage shape. Wrap each roll tightly in kitchen foil, securing both ends. Poach in the simmering water for 20 minutes, remove with a slotted spoon and leave to cool completely.

✷ Meanwhile, preheat the oven to 190°C/375°F/Gas Mark 5. Put the vegetable oil in a roasting tin and heat in the oven. Remove the kitchen foil and wrap each roulade tightly in 3 pancetta rashers. Carefully roll in the hot oil, then roast in the oven for 25-30 minutes, turning twice, until they are browned and crisp.

✷ Remove the roulades from the tin and keep warm. Place the tin on the hob, add the flour and stir well with a wooden spoon to form a smooth paste. Gradually whisk in the wine and stock. Leave to bubble for 4-5 minutes, then season to taste. Slice the roulades and serve with rösti and gravy.

# Traditional

## *Roast Chicken*

**SERVES 6**

one 2.25-kg/5-lb free-range
   chicken
55 g/2 oz butter
2 tbsp chopped fresh lemon thyme
1 lemon, quartered
125 ml/4 fl oz white wine
salt and pepper
6 fresh thyme sprigs, to garnish

★ Preheat the oven to 220°C/425°F/Gas Mark 7. Make sure the chicken is clean, wiping it inside and out with kitchen paper, and place in a roasting tin. In a bowl, soften the butter with a fork, mix in the thyme and season well with salt and pepper. Butter the chicken all over with the herb butter, inside and out, and place the lemon pieces inside the body cavity. Pour the wine over the chicken.

★ Roast in the centre of the preheated oven for 20 minutes. Reduce the temperature to 190°C/375°F/Gas Mark 5 and roast for a further 1¼ hours, basting frequently. Cover with foil if the skin begins to brown too much. If the tin dries out, add a little more wine or water.

★ Test that the chicken is cooked by piercing the thickest part of the leg with a sharp knife or skewer and making sure the juices run clear. Remove from the oven. Transfer the chicken to a warmed serving plate, cover loosely with foil and leave to rest for 10 minutes before carving. Place the roasting tin on the top of the stove and bubble the pan juices gently over a low heat until they have reduced and are thick and glossy. Season to taste with salt and pepper. Serve the chicken with the pan juices and scatter with the thyme sprigs.

**COOK'S NOTE**

★ Chicken has become a well-established favourite in recent years, although it was once seen as quite exclusive. Simply roasted, with plenty of thyme and lemon, chicken produces a succulent gastronomic feast for many occasions. You can stuff your chicken with a traditional stuffing, such as sage and onion, or with fruit like apricots and prunes, but often the best way is to keep it simple. If you do stuff the chicken, remember to stuff just the neck end, not the whole cavity, or the bird might not cook all the way through.

# Herbed Salmon with
## *Hollandaise Sauce*

SERVES 4

4 salmon fillets, about 175 g/
   6 oz each, skin removed
2 tbsp olive oil
1 tbsp chopped fresh dill
1 tbsp snipped fresh chives,
   plus extra to garnish
salt and pepper

HOLLANDAISE SAUCE
3 egg yolks
1 tbsp water
225 g/8 oz butter, cut into
   small cubes
juice of 1 lemon
salt and pepper

TO SERVE
freshly cooked sprouting broccoli
sesame seeds

✳ Preheat the grill to medium. Rinse the fish fillets under cold running water and pat dry with kitchen paper. Season to taste with salt and pepper. Combine the oil with the dill and chives in a bowl, then brush the mixture over the fish. Transfer to the grill and cook for 6-8 minutes, turning once and brushing with more oil and herb mixture, until cooked to your taste.

✳ Meanwhile, make the sauce. Put the egg yolks in a heatproof bowl over a saucepan of gently simmering water (or use a double boiler). Add the water and season to taste with salt and pepper. Reduce the heat until the water in the saucepan is barely simmering and whisk constantly until the mixture begins to thicken. Whisk in the butter, one piece at a time, until the mixture is thick and shiny. Whisk in the lemon juice, then remove from the heat.

✳ Remove the salmon from the grill and transfer to warmed individual serving plates. Pour the sauce over the fish and garnish with snipped fresh chives. Serve immediately on a bed of sprouting broccoli, garnished with sesame seeds.

**COOK'S NOTE**

✳ Do not allow the base of the bowl to touch the surface of the water when you are making the sauce, or the egg yolks may curdle. It is also important that the water is barely simmering rather than boiling vigorously.

# Mixed Nut Roast with

## *Cranberry Sauce*

SERVES 4

2 tbsp butter, plus extra
   for greasing
2 garlic cloves, chopped
1 large onion, chopped
50 g/1¾ oz pine kernels, toasted
75 g/2¾ oz hazelnuts, toasted
50 g/1¾ oz walnuts, ground
50 g/1¾ oz cashew nuts, ground
100 g/3½ oz fresh wholemeal
   breadcrumbs
1 egg, lightly beaten
2 tbsp chopped fresh thyme
250 ml/9 fl oz vegetable stock
salt and pepper
fresh thyme sprigs, to garnish
cooked sprouts, to serve

CRANBERRY SAUCE
175 g/6 oz fresh cranberries
100 g/3½ oz caster sugar
300 ml/10 fl oz red wine
1 cinnamon stick

★ Preheat the oven to 180°C/350°F/Gas Mark 4. Grease a loaf tin with butter and line it with greaseproof paper. Melt the remaining butter in a saucepan over a medium heat. Add the garlic and onion and cook, stirring, for 5 minutes, until softened. Remove from the heat. Grind the pine kernels and hazelnuts. Stir all the nuts into the saucepan, add the breadcrumbs, egg, thyme and stock and season to taste with salt and pepper.

★ Spoon the mixture into the loaf tin and level the surface. Cook in the preheated oven for 30 minutes, or until cooked through and golden. The loaf is cooked when a skewer inserted into the centre comes out clean.

★ Halfway through the cooking time, make the sauce. Put all the ingredients in a saucepan and bring to the boil. Reduce the heat and simmer gently, stirring occasionally, for 15 minutes.

★ To serve, remove the sauce from the heat and discard the cinnamon stick. Remove the nut roast from the oven and turn out onto a warmed serving dish. Garnish with thyme sprigs and serve with the sprouts and sauce.

**COOK'S NOTE**

★ Nuts contain a lot of oil and will turn rancid if they are stored too long. Buy them in small quantities, store in airtight containers and keep an eye on the 'use by' dates. It is probably worth buying fresh nuts for this festive treat.

# Steak with Pancakes & *Mustard Sauce*

SERVES 6

vegetable oil, for frying
6 fillet steaks, about
    150 g/5½ oz each
1 tbsp olive oil
1 tsp unsalted butter
200 ml/7 fl oz crème fraîche
2 tsp wholegrain mustard
2 tbsp snipped fresh chives
salt and pepper

PANCAKES
400 g/14 oz potatoes
55 g/2 oz self-raising flour
½ tsp baking powder
200 ml/7 fl oz milk
2 eggs, beaten

★ To make the pancakes, cook the potatoes in their skins in a large saucepan of boiling water until tender. Drain and leave until cool enough to handle. Peel, then pass through a potato ricer, or mash and press through a sieve, into a bowl.

★ Sift the flour and baking powder over the potatoes, then add a little of the milk and mix well. Add the remaining milk and the eggs and beat well to make a smooth batter.

★ Heat a little vegetable oil in a 20-cm/8-inch non-stick frying pan over a medium heat. Add a ladleful of the batter to cover the base of the pan and cook until little bubbles appear on the surface. Turn over and cook for a further minute, or until nicely browned, then turn out and keep warm. Repeat until you have cooked 6 pancakes.

★ Season the steaks to taste with salt and pepper. Heat the olive oil and butter in a non-stick frying pan over a high heat until sizzling. Add the fillet steaks and cook to your liking, then remove from the pan and keep warm. Add the crème fraîche and mustard to the pan, stir and heat through. Season well with salt and pepper. Serve each steak with a folded pancake and some sauce, scattered with a few snipped chives.

**COOK'S NOTE**

★ The pancakes can also make a vegetarian or non-meat main course, stuffed with some creamed spinach or smoked fish and soured cream.

# Apple & Date
## *Chutney*

MAKES ONE 300-G/10½-OZ JAR

175 ml/6 fl oz cider vinegar
1 shallot, finely chopped
1 cooking apple, peeled, cored
   and chopped
¼ tsp ground allspice
300 g/10½ oz Medjool dates,
   stoned and chopped
5 tbsp honey

★ Put the vinegar, shallot, apple and allspice in a saucepan and bring to the boil. Reduce the heat and simmer for 5-8 minutes. Add the dates and honey and cook for 8-10 minutes until the dates are soft and the liquid is syrupy.

★ Remove from the heat and leave to cool. Serve straight away or pack into sterilized jars and store in the refrigerator.

**COOK'S NOTE**

★ Chutney makes a lovely Christmas gift. Simply tie a ribbon around the lid of the jar and add a decorative label with the date you made it – it will last for 6 weeks in the refrigerator.

# Festive Jewelled *Rice*

SERVES 6

250 g/9 oz basmati rice
70 g/2½ oz red or wild rice
70 g/2½ oz ready-to-eat
  dried apricots
25 g/1 oz almonds, blanched
25 g/1 oz hazelnuts, toasted
1 fresh red chilli, deseeded and
  finely chopped
seeds of 1 pomegranate
1 tbsp finely chopped fresh parsley
1 tbsp finely chopped fresh mint
1 tbsp finely snipped fresh chives
2 tbsp white wine vinegar
6 tbsp extra virgin olive oil
1 shallot, finely chopped
salt and pepper

★ Cook the two types of rice separately according to the packet instructions. Drain and leave to cool, then tip into a large bowl.

★ Chop the apricots and nuts and add to the rice with the chilli, pomegranate seeds and the herbs. Mix together well.

★ Just before you are ready to serve, whisk the vinegar, oil and shallot together in a jug and season well with salt and pepper. Pour the dressing over the rice and mix well. Pile into a serving dish.

**COOK'S NOTE**

★ You can use other dried fruits or nuts in this dish and exclude the chilli if you prefer. Top with a few sliced salad onions for extra crunch.

# Wild Mushroom
## *Filo Parcels*

SERVES 6

30 g/1 oz dried porcini mushrooms
70 g/2½ oz butter
1 shallot, finely chopped
1 garlic clove, crushed
100 g/3½ oz chestnut
   mushrooms, sliced
100 g/3½ oz white cap
   mushrooms, sliced
200 g/7 oz wild mushrooms,
   roughly chopped
150 g/5½ oz basmati rice,
   cooked and cooled
2 tbsp dry sherry
1 tbsp soy sauce or
   mushroom sauce
1 tbsp chopped fresh
   flat-leaf parsley
18 sheets filo pastry,
   thawed if frozen
vegetable oil, for oiling
350 ml/12 fl oz crème fraîche
50 ml/2 fl oz Madeira
salt and pepper

★ Put the dried mushrooms in a heatproof bowl and just cover with boiling water. Leave to soak for 20 minutes.

★ Meanwhile, melt half the butter in a large frying pan over a low heat, add the shallot and garlic and cook, stirring occasionally, for 5-8 minutes until the shallot is transparent and soft. Add all the fresh mushrooms and cook, stirring, for 2-3 minutes.

★ Preheat the oven to 200°C/400°F/Gas Mark 6. Drain the dried mushrooms, reserving the soaking liquid, roughly chop and add to the frying pan with the rice, sherry, soy sauce and parsley. Season well with salt and pepper, mix together well and simmer until most of the liquid has evaporated.

★ Melt the remaining butter in a small saucepan. Lay 1 sheet of filo pastry on a work surface and brush with melted butter. Put another sheet on top and brush with butter, then top with a third sheet. Spoon some of the mushroom mixture into the centre, then fold in the edges to form a parcel. Use a little more of the melted butter to make sure that the edges are secure. Repeat to make 6 parcels.

★ Place the parcels on a lightly oiled baking sheet and brush with the remaining melted butter. Bake in the preheated oven for 25-30 minutes until golden.

★ Meanwhile, to make the sauce, heat the reserved soaking liquid in a saucepan, add the crème fraîche and Madeira and stir over a low heat until heated through. Season to taste with salt and pepper and serve with the parcels.

# Parsnip & Potato
## *Rösti*

SERVES 6

2 large potatoes
2 parsnips
olive oil, goose fat or lard,
    for frying
salt and pepper

★ Peel and grate the potatoes and parsnips on to a clean tea towel. Squeeze out any excess liquid, then spread out on to another clean tea towel or kitchen paper and leave to stand for 10 minutes.

★ Put the potatoes and parsnips in a bowl, mix together and season to taste with salt and pepper. Heat a little oil in a non-stick frying pan over a medium-high heat. Add a spoonful of the potato mixture, flatten with the back of a spoon to form a rösti and cook for 3–5 minutes until brown and crisp. Carefully turn over and cook for a further 2–3 minutes. Remove and drain on kitchen paper. Keep warm while you cook the remaining parsnip and potato mixture.

**COOK'S NOTE**

★ Rösti are also delicious for breakfast with a poached egg and some grilled pancetta, or with smoked salmon and soured cream and chives.

# Perfect Roast

## *Potatoes*

SERVES 8

70 g/2½ oz goose or duck fat
    or 5 tbsp olive oil
1 kg/2 lb 4 oz even-sized potatoes,
    peeled
coarse sea salt
8 fresh rosemary sprigs,
    to garnish

★ Preheat the oven to 230°C/450°F/Gas Mark 8. Put the fat in a large roasting tin, sprinkle generously with sea salt and place in the oven.

★ Meanwhile, cook the potatoes in a large saucepan of boiling water for 8-10 minutes until par-boiled. Drain well and, if the potatoes are large, cut them in half. Return the potatoes to the empty saucepan and shake vigorously to roughen their outsides.

★ Arrange the potatoes in a single layer in the hot fat and roast for 45 minutes. If they look as if they are beginning to char around the edges, reduce the oven temperature to 200°C/400°F/Gas Mark 6. Turn the potatoes over and roast for a further 30 minutes until crisp. Serve garnished with rosemary sprigs.

**COOK'S NOTE**

★ Use floury potatoes, such as King Edward or Maris Piper, for roasting, because these have the best texture. Do not allow them to stand around once they are cooked, or the outsides will turn leathery instead of crisp.

# Sugar-glazed

## *Parsnips*

SERVES 8

24 small parsnips, peeled
about 1 tsp salt
115 g/4 oz butter
115 g/4 oz soft brown sugar

★ Place the parsnips in a saucepan, add just enough water to cover, then add the salt. Bring to the boil, reduce the heat, cover and simmer for 20–25 minutes, until tender. Drain well.

★ Melt the butter in a heavy frying pan or wok. Add the parsnips and toss well. Sprinkle with the sugar, then cook, stirring frequently to prevent the sugar from sticking to the pan or burning. Cook the parsnips for 10–15 minutes, until golden and glazed. Transfer to a warm serving dish and serve immediately.

**COOK'S NOTE**

★ When buying parsnips, look for firm roots with no rusty patches and no damage to the skin. Store them in a cool, well-ventilated place for up to 5 days. Try to buy parsnips that are all about the same size, for even cooking.

# Spiced Winter *Vegetables*

**SERVES 4**

4 parsnips, scrubbed and
    trimmed but left unpeeled
4 carrots, scrubbed and
    trimmed but left unpeeled
2 onions, quartered
1 red onion, quartered
3 leeks, trimmed and cut
    into 6-cm/2½-inch slices
6 garlic cloves, left unpeeled
    and whole
6 tbsp extra virgin olive oil
½ tsp mild chilli powder
pinch of paprika
salt and pepper

★ Preheat the oven to 220°C/425°F/Gas Mark 7. Bring a large saucepan of water to the boil.

★ Cut the parsnips and carrots into wedges of similar size. Add them to the saucepan and cook for 5 minutes. Drain thoroughly and place in an ovenproof dish with the onions, leeks and garlic. Pour over the oil, sprinkle in the spices and salt and pepper to taste, then mix until all the vegetables are well coated.

★ Roast in the preheated oven for at least 1 hour. Turn the vegetables from time to time until they are tender and starting to colour. Remove from the oven, transfer to a warmed serving dish and serve immediately.

**COOK'S NOTE**

★ Providing there is room in the oven, these vegetables are ideal for Christmas lunch, because they offer a selection of different flavours without taking up the entire hob and several saucepans.

# Chestnut & Sausage

## *Stuffing*

**SERVES 6–8**

225 g/8 oz pork sausage meat
225 g/8 oz unsweetened
    chestnut purée
85 g/3 oz walnuts, chopped
115 g/4 oz ready-to-eat dried
    apricots, chopped
2 tbsp chopped fresh parsley
2 tbsp snipped fresh chives
2 tsp chopped fresh sage
4–5 tbsp double cream
salt and pepper

★ Combine the sausage meat and chestnut purée in a bowl, then stir in the walnuts, apricots, parsley, chives and sage. Stir in enough cream to make a firm, but not dry, mixture. Season to taste with salt and pepper.

★ If you are planning to stuff a turkey or goose, fill the neck cavity only to ensure the bird cooks all the way through. It is safer and more reliable to cook the stuffing separately, either rolled into small balls and placed on a baking sheet or spooned into an ovenproof dish.

★ Cook the separate stuffing in a preheated oven for 30-40 minutes at 190°C/375°F/Gas Mark 5. It should be allowed a longer time to cook if you are roasting a bird at a lower temperature in the same oven.

**COOK'S NOTE**

★ The combination of nuts, fruit and herbs in this stuffing helps to counteract the richness of traditional Christmas poultry, such as turkey and goose. It also produces an appetizing aroma during cooking.

# Cranberry

# *Sauce*

SERVES 8

thinly pared rind and juice
of 1 lemon
thinly pared rind and juice
of 1 orange
350 g/12 oz cranberries,
thawed if frozen
140 g/5 oz caster sugar
2 tbsp arrowroot, mixed
with 3 tbsp cold water

Cut the strips of lemon and orange rind into thin shreds and place in a heavy-based saucepan. If using fresh cranberries, rinse well and remove any stalks. Add the berries, citrus juice and sugar to the saucepan and cook over a medium heat, stirring occasionally, for 5 minutes, or until the berries begin to burst.

Strain the juice into a clean saucepan and reserve the cranberries. Stir the arrowroot mixture into the juice, then bring to the boil, stirring constantly, until the sauce is smooth and thickened. Remove from the heat and stir in the reserved cranberries.

Transfer the cranberry sauce to a bowl and leave to cool, then cover with clingfilm and chill in the refrigerator.

**COOK'S NOTE**

Turkey and cranberry sauce make a classic Christmas partnership. However, cranberry sauce can also be served to good effect with game, roast duck or chicken, or even some oily fish.

# Party Food & Drinks

# Mulled Ale &
## *Mulled Wine*

**MULLED ALE**
MAKES 2.8 LITRES/5 PINTS

2.5 litres/4½ pints strong ale
300 ml/10 fl oz brandy
2 tbsp caster sugar
large pinch of ground cloves
large pinch of ground ginger


**MULLED WINE**
MAKES 3.3 LITRES/5¾ PINTS

5 oranges
50 cloves
thinly pared rind and juice
   of 4 lemons
850 ml/1½ pints water
115 g/4 oz caster sugar
2 cinnamon sticks
2 litres/3½ pints red wine
150 ml/5 fl oz brandy

### *Mulled Ale*

★ Put all the ingredients in a heavy-based saucepan and heat gently, stirring, until the sugar has dissolved. Continue to heat so that it is simmering but not boiling. Remove the saucepan from the heat and serve the ale immediately in heatproof glasses.

### *Mulled Wine*

★ Prick the skins of 3 of the oranges all over with a fork and stud with the cloves, then set aside. Thinly pare the rind and squeeze the juice from the remaining oranges.

★ Put the orange rind and juice, lemon rind and juice, water, sugar and cinnamon in a heavy-based saucepan and bring to the boil over a medium heat, stirring occasionally, until the sugar has dissolved. Boil for 2 minutes without stirring, then remove from the heat, stir once and leave to stand for 10 minutes. Strain the liquid into a heatproof jug, pressing down on the contents of the sieve to extract all the juice.

★ Pour the wine into a separate saucepan and add the strained spiced juices, the brandy and the clove-studded oranges. Simmer gently without boiling, then remove the saucepan from the heat. Strain into heatproof glasses and serve the mulled wine immediately.

# Cheese
## *Straws*

**MAKES 10–12**

115 g/4 oz unsalted butter, plus
   extra for greasing
115 g/4 oz plain flour, plus extra
   for dusting
pinch of salt
pinch of paprika
1 tsp mustard powder
85 g/3 oz Cheddar or Gruyère
   cheese, grated
1 egg, lightly beaten
1–2 tbsp cold water
poppy seeds, for coating

★ Preheat the oven to 200°C/400°F/Gas Mark 6. Lightly grease 2 baking sheets with butter.

★ Sift the flour, salt, paprika and mustard powder into a bowl. Add the remaining butter, cut it into the flour with a knife, then rub in with your fingertips until the mixture resembles breadcrumbs. Stir in the cheese and add half of the beaten egg, then mix in enough water to make a firm dough. The dough may be stored in the freezer. Thaw at room temperature before rolling out.

★ Spread out the poppy seeds on a plate. Turn the dough on to a lightly floured work surface and knead briefly, then roll out. Using a sharp knife, cut into strips measuring 10 x 0.5 cm/4 x ¼ inch. Brush with the remaining beaten egg and roll the straws in the poppy seeds to coat, then arrange them on the baking sheets. Gather up the dough trimmings and re-roll. To make pastry rings, stamp out 10–12 rounds with a 6-cm/2½-inch cutter, then stamp out the centres with a 5-cm/2-inch cutter. Brush with the egg and place on the baking sheets.

★ Bake in the preheated oven for 10 minutes until golden brown. Leave the cheese straws on the baking sheets to cool slightly, then transfer to wire racks to cool completely. Store in an airtight container. Thread the pastry straws through the pastry rings before serving.

**COOK'S NOTE**

★ Rather than using poppy seeds, you can brush the cheese straws with mild mustard and sprinkle with a little cayenne pepper before baking. Be careful not to make them too spicy.

# Scallops Wrapped
## *in Pancetta*

SERVES 12

12 fresh rosemary sprigs
6 raw scallops, corals removed
12 thin-cut pancetta rashers
salt and pepper

DRESSING
2 tbsp olive oil
1 tbsp white wine vinegar
1 tsp honey

★ First prepare the rosemary by stripping most of the leaves off the stalks, leaving a cluster of leaves at the top. Trim the stalks to about 6 cm/2½ inches long, cutting each tip at the base end at an angle.

★ Cut each scallop in half through the centre to give 2 discs of scallop, wrap each one in a pancetta rasher and, keeping the end tucked under, place on a plate. Cover and chill in the refrigerator for 15 minutes.

★ To make the dressing, whisk the oil, vinegar and honey together in a small bowl and season to taste with salt and pepper.

★ Preheat the grill to high or heat a ridged griddle pan over a high heat. Cook the scallops under the grill or on the griddle pan for 2 minutes on each side until the pancetta is crisp and brown. Spear each one on a prepared rosemary skewer and serve hot, with the dressing as a dip.

**COOK'S NOTE**
★ These could be served alongside cocktail sausages and angels on horseback (oysters wrapped in pancetta) as delicious hot party snacks.

# Piquant Crab
## *Bites*

MAKES 50

100 g/3½ oz fresh white
    breadcrumbs
2 large eggs, separated
200 ml/7 fl oz crème fraîche
1 tsp English mustard powder
500 g/1 lb 2 oz fresh
    white crabmeat
1 tbsp chopped fresh dill
groundnut oil, for frying
salt and pepper
2 limes, quartered, to serve

★ Tip the breadcrumbs into a large bowl. In a separate bowl, whisk the egg yolks with the crème fraîche and mustard powder and add to the breadcrumbs with the crabmeat and dill, season to taste with salt and pepper and mix together well. Cover and chill in the refrigerator for 15 minutes.

★ In a clean bowl, whisk the egg whites until stiff. Lightly fold a tablespoonful of the egg whites into the crab mixture, then fold in the remaining egg whites.

★ Heat 2 tablespoons of oil in a non-stick frying pan over a medium-high heat. Drop in as many teaspoonfuls of the crab mixture as will fit in the frying pan without overcrowding, flatten slightly and cook for 2 minutes, or until brown and crisp. Flip over and cook for a further 1–2 minutes until the undersides are browned. Remove and drain on kitchen paper. Keep warm while you cook the remaining crab mixture, adding more oil to the frying pan if necessary.

★ Serve the crab bites warm with the lime quarters for squeezing over.

## COOK'S NOTE

★ These can be made in advance and reheated in a medium oven. They also freeze well, in which case they should be cooked, cooled and then frozen. Thaw thoroughly before reheating.

# Leek & Bacon *Tartlets*

MAKES 12

**PASTRY**
225 g/8 oz plain flour
pinch of salt
½ tsp paprika
100 g/3½ oz unsalted butter,
    chilled and diced, plus extra
    for greasing

**FILLING**
25 g/1 oz unsalted butter
1 tsp olive oil
1 leek, trimmed and chopped
8 unsmoked streaky bacon
    rashers, cut into lardons
2 eggs, beaten
150 ml/5 fl oz double cream
1 tsp snipped fresh chives
salt and pepper

✴ Lightly grease a 7.5-cm/3-inch, 12-hole muffin tin with butter. Sift the flour, salt and paprika into a bowl and rub in the remaining butter until the mixture resembles breadcrumbs. Add a very little cold water – just enough to bring the dough together. Knead the dough briefly on a floured work surface.

✴ Divide the pastry in half. Roll out 1 piece of pastry and, using a 9-cm/3½-inch plain cutter, cut out 6 rounds, then roll each round into a 12-cm/4½-inch round. Repeat with the other half of the pastry until you have 12 rounds, then use to line the muffin tin. Cover and chill in the refrigerator for 30 minutes.

✴ Meanwhile, preheat the oven to 200°C/400°F/Gas Mark 6. To make the filling, melt the butter with the oil in a non-stick frying pan over a medium heat, add the leek and cook, stirring frequently, for 5 minutes until soft. Remove with a slotted spoon and set aside. Add the lardons to the frying pan and cook for 5 minutes, or until crisp. Remove and drain on kitchen paper.

✴ Line the pastry cases with baking paper and baking beans and bake in the preheated oven for 10 minutes. Whisk the eggs and cream together in a bowl, season to taste with salt and pepper, then stir in the chives with the cooked leek and bacon. Remove the pastry cases from the oven and carefully lift out the paper and beans. Divide the bacon and leek mixture between the pastry cases and bake for 10 minutes until the tarts are golden and risen. Leave to cool in the tin for 5 minutes, then carefully transfer to a wire rack. Serve warm or cold.

# Corn & Parmesan *Fritters*

**MAKES 25-30**

5 fresh corn on the cob
    or 500 g/1 lb 2 oz frozen or
    canned sweetcorn kernels
2 eggs, beaten
4 tbsp plain flour
2 tbsp finely grated
    Parmesan cheese
1 tsp bicarbonate of soda
4 tbsp full-fat milk
vegetable oil, for frying
salt

★ If you are using fresh corn on the cobs, cook them in a large saucepan of boiling water for 7 minutes, then drain well. Stand them on their ends, cut away the kernels and leave to cool. If using frozen sweetcorn kernels, leave to thaw first, or drain canned sweetcorn kernels.

★ Put the sweetcorn kernels in a bowl with the eggs, flour, Parmesan cheese, bicarbonate of soda and a pinch of salt. Mix together, then add the milk and stir together well.

★ Heat the oil to a depth of 4 cm/1½ inches in a deep saucepan to a temperature of 180-190°C/350-375°F, or until a cube of bread browns in 30 seconds. Drop 4 teaspoonfuls of the mixture into the oil at a time and cook for 2 minutes. Turn over and cook for a further minute or so, or until crisp, brown and slightly puffed up. Remove and drain on kitchen paper. Keep warm while you cook the remaining batches of mixture - you may need to add a little more oil between batches and scoop out any stray sweetcorn kernels. Sprinkle with salt to serve.

**COOK'S NOTE**

★ You could replace the Parmesan cheese with ½ teaspoon of either paprika or chilli powder for extra bite.

# Smoked Turkey &

## *Stuffing Parcels*

MAKES 12

12 slices smoked turkey breast
4 tbsp cranberry sauce or jelly
400 g/14 oz cooked and cooled
    sausage-meat stuffing
24 sheets filo pastry, thawed
    if frozen
70 g/2½ oz butter, melted

★ Preheat the oven to 190°C/375°F/Gas Mark 5. Put a non-stick baking sheet into the oven to heat.

★ For each parcel, spread a slice of smoked turkey with a teaspoonful of cranberry sauce, spoon 35 g/1¼ oz of the stuffing into the centre and roll up the turkey slice. Lay 1 sheet of filo pastry on a work surface and brush with a little of the melted butter. Put another sheet on top, then put the rolled-up turkey in the centre. Add a little more cranberry sauce, then carefully fold the filo pastry around the turkey, tucking under the ends to form a neat parcel. Repeat to make 12 parcels.

★ Place the parcels on the hot baking sheet, brush with the remaining melted butter and bake in the preheated oven for 25 minutes until golden. Serve hot.

## COOK'S NOTE

★ You can add a few chopped chestnuts or other Christmas leftovers to these parcels, or replace the turkey with cooked chicken.

# Desserts &

# After-dinner Treats

# Gingered Brandy *Snaps*

MAKES 36

vegetable oil, for greasing
115 g/4 oz unsalted butter
140 g/5 oz golden syrup
115 g/4 oz Demerara sugar
115 g/4 oz plain flour
2 tsp ground ginger
600 ml/1 pint stiffly whipped
  double cream, to serve

 Preheat the oven to 160°C/325°F/Gas Mark 3. Brush a non-stick baking sheet with oil. Place the butter, syrup and sugar in a saucepan and set over a low heat, stirring occasionally, until melted and combined. Remove the saucepan from the heat and leave to cool slightly. Sift the flour and ground ginger together into the butter mixture and beat until smooth. Spoon 2 teaspoons of the mixture on to the baking sheet, spacing them well apart. Bake for 8 minutes until pale golden brown. Keep the remaining mixture warm. Meanwhile, oil the handle of a wooden spoon.

Remove the baking sheet from the oven and leave to stand for 1 minute so that the brandy snaps firm up slightly. Remove 1 with a palette knife and immediately curl it around the handle of the wooden spoon. Once set, carefully slide it off the handle and transfer to a wire rack to cool completely. Repeat with the other brandy snap. Bake the remaining mixture and shape in the same way, using a cool baking sheet each time. Do not be tempted to cook more, or the rounds will set before you have time to shape them. When all the brandy snaps are cool, store in an airtight container.

To serve, spoon the whipped cream into a piping bag fitted with a star nozzle. Fill the brandy snaps with cream from both ends.

## COOK'S NOTE

The unfilled brandy snaps will keep for at least a week in an airtight container. Do not fill them with cream until you are almost ready to serve, or they will become soggy and collapse as guests try to eat them.

# Traditional Brandy
## *Butter*

SERVES 6-8

115 g/4 oz unsalted butter,
   at room temperature
55 g/2 oz caster sugar
55 g/2 oz icing sugar, sifted
3 tbsp brandy

★ Cream the butter in a bowl until it is very smooth and soft. Gradually beat in both types of sugar. Add the brandy, a little at a time, beating well after each addition and taking care not to let the mixture curdle.

★ Spread out the butter on a sheet of foil, cover and chill in the refrigerator until firm. Keep chilled until ready to serve.

**COOK'S NOTE**

★ As an alternative, make a tasty rum butter. Beat the finely grated rind of 1 unwaxed orange into the butter with the two types of sugar and substitute dark or white rum for the brandy, adding it gradually to avoid curdling.

# Rich Christmas

## *Pudding*

SERVES 10-12

200 g/7 oz currants
200 g/7 oz raisins
200 g/7 oz sultanas
150 ml/5 fl oz sweet sherry
175 g/6 oz butter, plus extra
    for greasing
175 g/6 oz brown sugar
4 eggs, beaten
150 g/5½ oz self-raising flour
100 g/3½ oz fresh white or
    wholemeal breadcrumbs
50 g/1¾ oz blanched almonds,
    chopped
juice of 1 orange
grated rind of ½ orange
grated rind of ½ lemon
½ tsp mixed spice
holly, to decorate
icing sugar, for dusting

★ Put the currants, raisins and sultanas in a glass bowl and pour the sherry over. Cover and leave to soak for at least 2 hours.

★ Beat together the butter and brown sugar in a bowl. Beat in the eggs, then fold in the flour. Stir in the soaked fruit and the sherry with the breadcrumbs, almonds, orange juice and rind, lemon rind and mixed spice. Grease a 1.2-litre/ 2-pint pudding basin and spoon the mixture into it, packing it down well and leaving a gap of 2.5 cm/1 inch at the top. Cut a round of greaseproof paper 3 cm/1¼ inches larger than the top of the basin, grease with butter and place over the pudding. Secure with string, then top with 2 layers of foil. Place the pudding in a saucepan filled with boiling water that reaches two-thirds of the way up the basin. Reduce the heat and simmer for 6 hours, topping up the water in the saucepan when necessary.

★ Remove from the heat and leave to cool. Renew the greaseproof paper and foil and store in the refrigerator for 2-8 weeks. To reheat, steam as before for 2 hours. Decorate with holly and a dusting of icing sugar.

**COOK'S NOTE**

★ If you have too much of the mixture and it fills the pudding basin, it is a good idea to make a pleat across the centre of the first greaseproof paper and foil rounds, to allow plenty of room for the pudding to expand during cooking. You don't need to pleat the second coverings.

# Christmas *Cake*

MAKES ONE 20-CM/8-INCH CAKE

150 g/5½ oz raisins
125 g/4½ oz stoned dried dates, chopped
125 g/4½ oz sultanas
100 g/3½ oz glacé cherries, rinsed
150 ml/5 fl oz brandy
225 g/8 oz butter, plus extra for greasing
200 g/7 oz caster sugar
4 eggs
grated rind of 1 orange
grated rind of 1 lemon
1 tbsp black treacle
225 g/8 oz plain flour
½ tsp salt
½ tsp baking powder
1 tsp mixed spice
25 g/1 oz toasted almonds, chopped
25 g/1 oz toasted hazelnuts, chopped
750 g/1 lb 10 oz marzipan
3 tbsp apricot jam, warmed
3 egg whites
650 g/1 lb 7 oz icing sugar
silver dragées, balls and ribbon, to decorate

★ Make this cake at least 3 weeks in advance. Put all the fruit in a bowl and pour over the brandy. Cover and leave to soak overnight.

★ Preheat the oven to 110°C/225°F/Gas Mark ¼. Grease a 20-cm/8-inch cake tin with butter and line it with greaseproof paper. Cream the remaining butter and the sugar in a bowl until fluffy. Gradually beat in the eggs. Stir in the citrus rind and treacle. Sift the flour, salt, baking powder and mixed spice into a separate bowl, then fold into the egg mixture. Fold in the soaked fruit and brandy and the nuts, then spoon the mixture into the cake tin.

★ Bake in the preheated oven for at least 3 hours. If it browns too quickly, cover with foil. The cake is cooked when a skewer inserted into the centre comes out clean. Remove from the oven and leave to cool on a wire rack. Store in an airtight container until required.

★ Roll out the marzipan and cut to shape to cover the top and sides of the cake. Brush the cake with the jam and press the marzipan on to the surface. Make the icing by placing the egg whites in a bowl and adding the icing sugar a little at a time, beating well until the icing is very thick and will stand up in peaks. Spread over the covered cake, using a fork to give texture. Decorate as you wish with silver dragées, balls and ribbon.

## COOK'S NOTE

★ While the cake is being stored prior to icing, you can pierce several holes in the top with a skewer and drizzle lightly with brandy, sherry, Madeira wine or maraschino liqueur once a week to add extra flavour and keep it moist.

# Dark Chocolate
# *Yule Log*

**SERVES 8**

butter, for greasing
150 g/5½ oz caster sugar, plus
    extra for sprinkling
115 g/4 oz self-raising flour,
    plus extra for dusting
4 eggs, separated
1 tsp almond extract
280 g/10 oz plain chocolate,
    broken into squares
225 ml/8 fl oz double cream
2 tbsp rum
holly, to decorate
icing sugar, for dusting

✸ Preheat the oven to 190°C/375°F/Gas Mark 5. Grease with butter and line a 40 x 28-cm/16 x 11-inch Swiss roll tin, then dust with flour.

✸ Reserve 2 tablespoons of the caster sugar and whisk the remainder with the egg yolks in a bowl until thick and pale. Stir in the almond extract. Whisk the egg whites in a separate grease-free bowl until soft peaks form. Gradually whisk in the reserved sugar until stiff and glossy. Sift half the flour over the egg yolk mixture and fold in, then fold in one-quarter of the egg whites. Sift and fold in the remaining flour, followed by the remaining egg whites. Spoon the mixture into the tin, spreading it out evenly with a palette knife. Bake in the preheated oven for 15 minutes, until lightly golden.

✸ Sprinkle caster sugar over a sheet of greaseproof paper and turn out the cake on to the paper. Roll up and leave to cool.

✸ Place the chocolate in a heatproof bowl. Bring the cream to boiling point in a small saucepan, then pour it over the chocolate and stir until the chocolate has melted. Beat with an electric mixer until smooth and thick. Reserve about one-third of the chocolate mixture and stir the rum into the remainder. Unroll the cake and spread the chocolate and rum mixture over. Re-roll and place on a plate or silver board. Spread the reserved chocolate mixture evenly over the top and sides. Mark with a fork so that the surface resembles tree bark. Just before serving, decorate with holly and a sprinkling of icing sugar to resemble snow.

# Sweet Pumpkin *Pie*

**SERVES 8**

### FILLING

1.8 kg/4 lb sweet pumpkin
400 ml/14 fl oz sweetened
   condensed milk
2 eggs
½ tsp ground cinnamon
½ tsp ground nutmeg
½ tsp ground cloves
½ tsp salt
½ tsp vanilla extract
1 tbsp Demerara sugar

### PASTRY

55 g/2 oz unsalted butter,
   chilled and diced, plus extra
   for greasing
140 g/5 oz plain flour, plus extra
   for dusting
¼ tsp baking powder
½ tsp ground cinnamon
¼ tsp ground nutmeg
¼ tsp ground cloves
½ tsp salt
50 g/1¾ oz caster sugar
1 egg

### STREUSEL TOPPING

2 tbsp plain flour
4 tbsp Demerara sugar
1 tsp ground cinnamon
2 tbsp unsalted butter,
   chilled and diced
75 g/2¾ oz pecan nuts, chopped
75 g/2¾ oz walnuts, chopped

Preheat the oven to 190°C/375°F/Gas Mark 5. Halve the pumpkin, remove and discard the seeds, stem and stringy insides. Put the pumpkin halves, face down, in a shallow baking tin and cover with foil. Bake in the preheated oven for 1½ hours, then leave to cool. Scoop out the flesh and mash with a potato masher or purée in a food processor. Drain away any excess liquid. Cover with clingfilm and chill until ready to use.

To make the pastry, grease a 23-cm/9-inch round pie dish with butter. Sift the flour and baking powder into a large bowl. Stir in spices, salt and caster sugar. Rub in the remaining butter until the mixture resembles fine breadcrumbs, then make a well in the centre. Lightly beat the egg and pour it into the well. Mix together with a wooden spoon, then use your hands to shape the dough into a ball. Roll out on a lightly floured work surface to a large round and use it to line the dish, then trim the edge. Cover with clingfilm and chill in the refrigerator for 30 minutes.

Preheat the oven to 220°C/425°F/Gas Mark 7. To make the filling, put the pumpkin purée in a large bowl, then stir in the condensed milk and the eggs. Add the spices and salt, then stir in the vanilla extract and Demerara sugar. Pour into the pastry case and bake for 15 minutes.

Meanwhile, make the topping. Combine the flour, sugar and cinnamon in a bowl, rub in the butter until crumbly, then stir in the nuts. Remove the pie from the oven and reduce the heat to 180°C/350°F/Gas Mark 4. Sprinkle the topping over the pie, then bake for a further 35 minutes. Serve hot or cold.

# Index

ale, mulled 64-5
apple & date chutney 44-5

bacon, & leek tartlets 72-3
brandy butter, traditional 82-3
brandy snaps, gingered 80-1
bread sauce 26-7

C

cake
    Christmas 86-7
    Yule log 88-9
cheese
    corn & Parmesan fritters
       74-5
    soufflés, double 22-3
    straws 66-7
chestnut & sausage stuffing 58-9
chicken
    roulades 34-5
    traditional roast 36-7
chocolate
    truffle selection 94-5
    Yule log 88-9
Christmas cake 86-7
Christmas pudding 84-5
chutney, apple & date 44-5
corn & Parmesan fritters 74-5
crab bites, piquant 70-1
cranberry
    roast squash 20-1

    sauce 40-1, 60-1
    smoked turkey & stuffing parcels
       76-7

date, & apple chutney 44-5
door wreath 10-1
duck with maderia & blueberry sauce
    32-3

goose with honey & pears 28-9

hollandaise sauce 38-9

leek & bacon tartlets 72-3

mince pies, festive 92-3
mushroom filo parcels, wild 48-9

napkin holders 8-9
nut roast with cranberry sauce
    40-1

parsnips
    & potato rösti 50-1
    sugar-glazed parsnips 54-5
pheasant with wine & herbs
    30-1

potato
    pancakes, with steak 42-3
    & parsnip rösti 50-1
    perfect roast potatoes 52-3
prawn cocktail 14-5
pudding, Christmas 84-5
pumpkin pie 90-1

rice, jewelled 46-7

salmon
    herbed with hollandaise sauce
       38-9
    risotto 18-9
sausage, & chestnut stuffing 58-9
scallops wrapped in Pancetta 68-9
squash with cranberries 20-1
steak with pancakes & mustard
    sauce 42-3
stuffing, chestnut & sausage 58-9

turkey
    with bread sauce 26-7
    club sandwiches 16-7
    & stuffing parcels 76-7

vegetables, spiced winter 56-7

wine, mulled 64-5

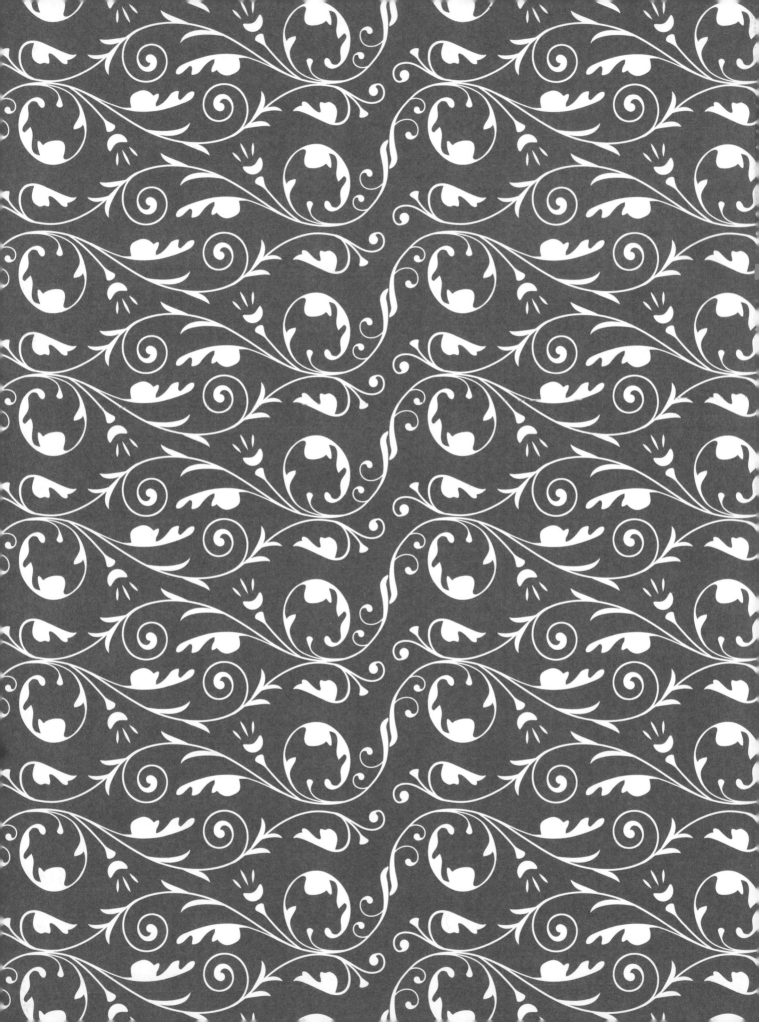